Our Moving Earth

Written by Anna Porter

Series Consultant: Linda Hoyt

WorldWise™
Content-based Learning

T0360031

Contents

Introduction

An earthquake can split the ground open in a few seconds. Giant waves called tsunamis can flood a coastline. Or there can be a vast explosion of steam or fireballs of rock and ash from a volcano as it erupts. Hot rock known as **lava** flows like a river of melted chocolate, and it can spread over the land or the ocean floor in a few minutes.

These are the furious forces of nature from deep within the earth's crust and they change the earth's surface. New mountains, canyons and holes called craters appear, and islands rise up from the ocean floor. Some changes happen so fast that they can cause great harm to people, wildlife and property.

Some changes happen slowly. They change over millions of years as mountains are pushed up and lakes form as parts of the earth sink.

Chapter 1

What is the earth made of?

If you could cut the earth in half you would see that it is not one big solid rock, but that it has three main layers of rock like the rings of an onion. These are called the crust, the mantle and the core. The deeper you go towards the centre of the earth, the hotter these rocks get.

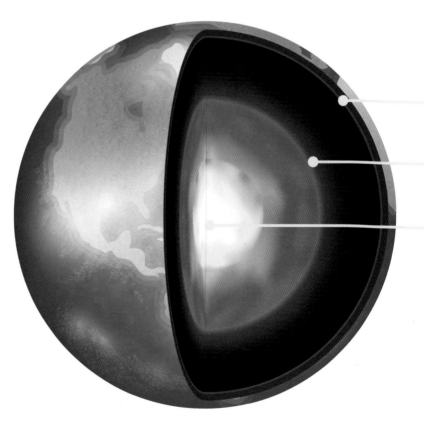

The crust. This is a thin layer of rocks that lies below the earth's **continents** and oceans.

The mantle.
This is a layer of hard, solid rock above the core.

The lines on this map show the earth's plates.

The core. This is the hottest part of the earth. The rock is so hot that it melts into a thick liquid called **magma**. It boils and bubbles.

The earth's crust and mantle are made up of seven huge rocky plates that float on top of the hot liquid rock in the layer underneath them. The plates are constantly and slowly moving.

How does rock in the earth's crust move?

The edges of the rocky plates move about two centimetres each year. The plates move apart, they move together, and sometimes they bang against each other or slide under one another. As a result, rocks of the crust may fold, bend or buckle.

Folding rocks

Sometimes huge blocks of rock can buckle like the bonnet of a car in a head-on collision. The buckled rock is pushed up and tilted in a particular direction to form a mountain range like the Rockies, the Andes or the Himalayas. Other parts of the crust cool and sink and fill with rainwater to become lakes or shallow seas.

The Andes, Peru

How a mountain range is formed

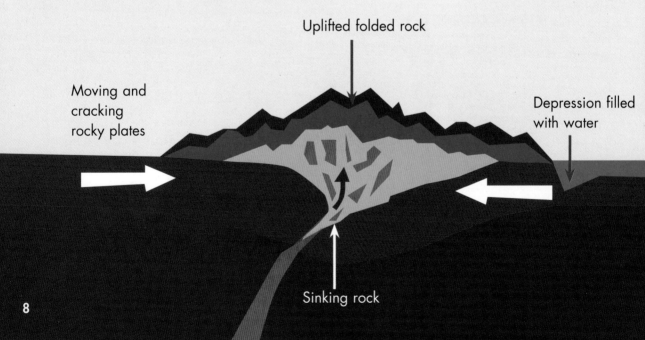

Uplifted folded rock

Moving and cracking rocky plates

Depression filled with water

Sinking rock

fault line in Iceland

A fault line in Utah, USA

Fault lines and cracking in the earth's crust

At other times when the edges of the plates meet and collide, the rocks are too brittle to fold, so they develop cracks in the earth's crust known as **fault lines**. Most of earth's earthquakes and volcanoes occur along fault lines.

Chapter 2

What happens during an earthquake?

Most earthquakes and **tremors** are so small that people do not feel them.

But if the tremors are powerful, huge cracks in the earth's surface break open or large areas of land can move downhill in the form of a landslide. If snowy mountains are nearby, the moving snow can crash down the mountain in an **avalanche**. Moving earth or snow can bury people, animals, plants and buildings.

A landslide

An avalanche

A large earthquake can cause buildings above the ground to move and fall. As buildings topple over, falling bricks, concrete, tin or tiles can crush people. Roads can be destroyed, trains derailed and cars crushed. Of all natural **hazards**, earthquakes can result in the greatest loss of life.

How do scientists measure the size of an earthquake?

Scientists called geologists study rocks and the movements of the Earth. They use machines to record and measure the size and strength of earth tremors on machines. The size of an earthquake is measured by the amount of energy it releases from under the ground. This is called the magnitude.

The measurements used have a range from one to eight. It is known as the Richter scale and was invented by Dr Charles Richter. The larger the number appearing on this scale, the greater the damage the earthquake will cause.

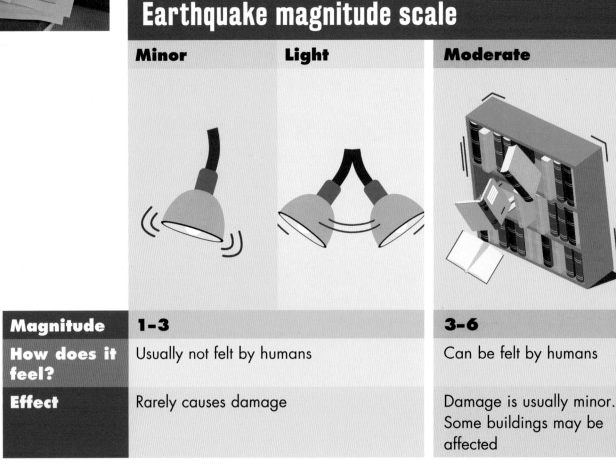

Earthquake magnitude scale

	Minor	Light	Moderate
Magnitude	1-3		3-6
How does it feel?	Usually not felt by humans		Can be felt by humans
Effect	Rarely causes damage		Damage is usually minor. Some buildings may be affected

An average earthquake lasts for less than one minute. Some have lasted for over four minutes. After an earthquake happens, there can be more earth movements and shaking called after-shocks. These can cause even more damage to buildings and roads.

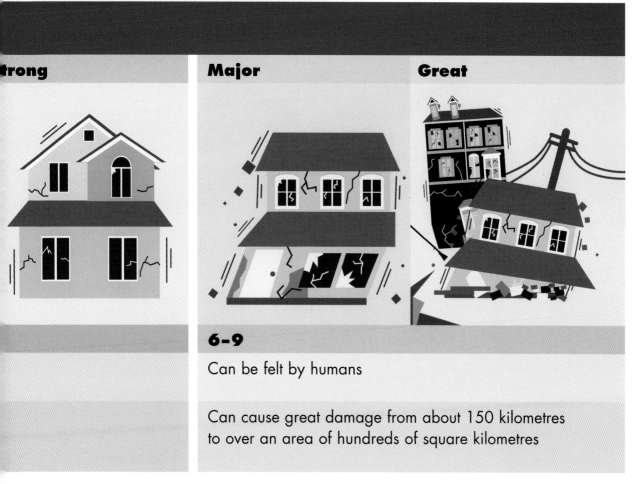

trong

Major

Great

6-9

Can be felt by humans

Can cause great damage from about 150 kilometres to over an area of hundreds of square kilometres

Tsunamis

If large-scale sudden earthquake tremors happen under the sea floor, they cause huge wave movements in the seawater called tsunamis. These waves rush across the surface of the ocean at speeds of up to 300 kilometres per hour and build up into a high wall of water. This wall can be up to 30 metres high, as high as a 10-storey building.

How far this wave wall reaches inland and what is in its path determine how dangerous it will be. Some tsunamis blasting onto the shore can reach over 10 kilometres inland, flooding everything in their path. Many fishing villages, coastal towns or tourist buildings can be devastated. The unique characteristics of tsunamis make them hard to predict, detect or monitor.

Find out more

Find out where the biggest earthquake occurred. What happened straight after it? What damage did it cause?

THE NEWS

26 December 2004

Indian Ocean Earthquake and Tsunami

More than 11,000 people in six countries were killed today when the most powerful earthquake in 40 years triggered huge tidal waves that hit coastlines across Asia, including in Sri Lanka, Indonesia, India, Thailand, Malaysia and the Maldives.

The quake occurred at a place where several huge geological plates push against each other with massive force. Waves as high as six metres crashed into coastal areas throughout the Indian Ocean and Andaman Sea. The US Geological Survey's website recorded the magnitude 8.9 earthquake 1,600 kilometres northwest of Jakarta on the island of Sumatra. The earthquake's centre was 40 kilometres below the seabed. Aftershocks struck around the range of magnitude seven. This earthquake was the fifth most powerful in the world since 1900.

Chapter 3

What are volcanoes?

When rock presses together or collides under the earth's crust, gases and **magma**, the extremely hot liquid rock, are forced up through cracks and a volcano is formed.

When the magma reaches the earth's surface, it is called **lava**. Sometimes the lava flows slowly out over the land, moves downhill, cools and hardens.

At other times, the erupting lava is like a gassy fireball. It explodes out of the crack with great speed and power, bringing with it ash, pieces of rock and soot. These shoot up into the **atmosphere** and spread over a wide area.

Volcanoes can continue to erupt and over time may produce other landforms: a crater, a dome, a mountain or an island.

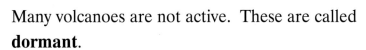
Magma is forced upwards and shoots out of the volcano

Find out more

Find out how volcanoes got their name.

Farmland near the volcano Mount Fuji, Japan

Many volcanoes are not active. These are called **dormant**.

Active volcanoes erupt from time to time. They cause most harm as a natural **hazard** when people live near them or develop farms on the rich soils formed from their lava.

Warnings about danger from volcanoes

Sensitive monitoring devices can now detect increasing volcanic activity months in advance of an eruption. The only effective method to prevent or lessen any harm is to communicate with local officials and the media about a possible **eruption**. These officials can warn people at risk and arrange for the evacuation of people and animals.

A dormant volcano, Iceland

17

Volcanic islands

Over millions of years, many island groups have been formed from volcanoes erupting under the seabed. The hot magma rises upwards until it spews out as lava through a weak place on the surface of the seafloor at what is called a hot spot. These hot spots can occur in the middle of a plate under the ocean. When the sizzling lava hits the cooler water, it hardens into an underwater volcano. Over time, and after many eruptions, the hardened lava on this volcano builds high enough to emerge above the ocean surface as an island.

Under all the earth's oceans there are more than one million underwater volcanoes. Of these, about 75,000 rise up nearly a kilometre above the ocean floor.

Find out more

Find out about other groups of islands in the Pacific Ocean that are formed from volcanoes.

Molten lava flowing into the ocean, Hawaii Island, US

Kauai Island on Hawaii, US

Hawaii, US

The islands of Hawaii have many active volcanoes. They were first formed over 70 million years ago. Way down on the ocean floor, a hot spot of magma began to gush lava into the sea. About 40 million years later, this lava built upwards to a height of 5,500 metres, forming bare volcanic islands rising out of the sea. These became the group of islands called Hawaii, and they are the most isolated in the world.

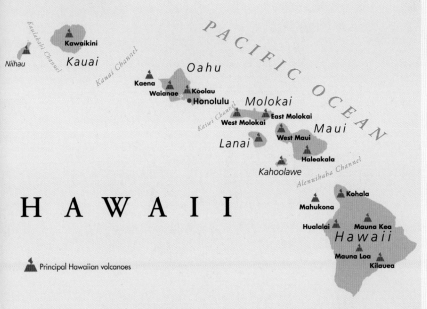

Kaulakahi Channel

Kawaikini

Niihau   Kauai

Kauai Channel

PACIFIC

Oahu

Kaena

Waianae   Koolau

Honolulu

Molokai

Kaiwi Channel

East Molokai

West Molokai

Maui

OCEAN

Lanai

West Maui

Haleakala

Kahoolawe

Alenuihaha Channel

HAWAII

Kohala

Mahukona

Hualalai   Mauna Kea

Hawaii

Mauna Loa

Kilauea

▲ Principal Hawaiian volcanoes

Find out more

There are three active volcanoes in Hawaii. On Hawaii Island, the Kilauea Caldera continues to show hot slabs of recent lava flows. It has been erupting constantly since 1983. At that time, lava shot up 30 metres and covered about 50 hectares. Where are the other two active volcanoes in Hawaii?

19

Volcanic craters

After they have erupted several times, some old volcanoes have very large holes, or craters, in their tops. As the magma has moved up through the earth's surface, the empty hole that is left cannot support the walls of the mountain above it. These walls collapse and form a large crater. Some craters can be over 90 metres wide. These often fill with water and are called crater lakes or **calderas**. The steep high walls of the crater form a circle around and above the water of the lake.

Find out more

Find out about crater lakes in Australia.

Castle Geyser erupts with hot water and steam.

Geothermal hot springs, Yellowstone National Park

Island Park Caldera, Yellowstone, US

Streaming geysers near Yellowstone River

Yellowstone in the United States contains one of the world's largest volcanic craters, the Island Park Caldera. This crater was formed about two million years ago, when a volcano erupted, spewing liquid lava, boulders and soot into the atmosphere. Scientists are now studying the buildup of the magma in the hole beneath this crater. The ground in the crater has been surveyed, and the magma chamber is 70 kilometres long and 45 kilometres wide. This magma seems to be again bulging upwards towards the earth's surface. Scientists are trying to predict when this volcano may erupt again.

Find out more

Find something that would be as big in size as this magma pool in the Island Park Caldera.

Find out more
What countries in the world have geysers? Can you name them?

Volcanic hot springs and geysers

Other landforms caused by volcanoes are hot springs and geysers.

Freshwater can seep down through cracks in rocks below the earth's surface. When it comes in contact with the hot rocks near volcanoes, the water heats up very quickly. The hot water builds up pressure and steam, and eventually shoots upwards through a tiny crack in the earth's surface.

If this hot water or steam flows out of the surface and forms a pool, it is called a hot spring. If the temperature of the underground water becomes extremely hot, the pressure forces huge jets of water and steam to shoot up high into the air. This is called a geyser. The water inside a geyser can be three times as hot as water boiling in a kettle.

How geysers and hot springs form

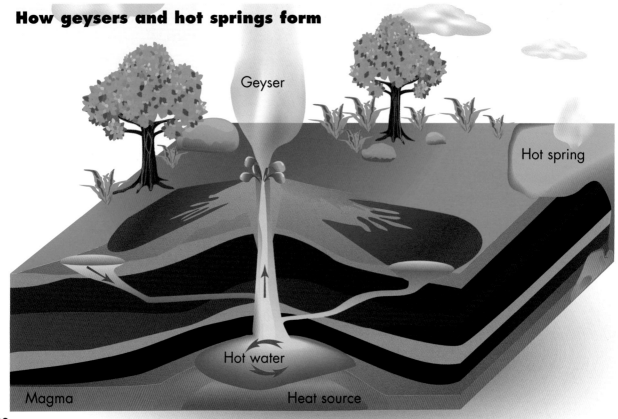

Geyser

Hot spring

Hot water

Magma

Heat source

One of the most famous geysers is in the United States of America. It is called Old Faithful. It shoots boiling steam and water up to 55 metres into the air.

Think about ...

Why is this geyser called Old Faithful?

Old Faithful geyser erupts

Areas around Rotorua in New Zealand are famous for their large geysers and hot springs. The Pohutu geyser is the largest in New Zealand. It erupts up to 15 times a day and shoots steam and boiling water 30 metres skyward.

Pohutu geyser

23

Chapter 4

Where do large earthquakes and volcanoes occur?

The moving rocky plates that cause large earthquakes and volcanoes occur in particular zones around the world.

The Pacific Ocean Ring of Fire

Japan

Pacific Ocean

Hawa

Indonesia

Papua New Guinea

Australia

New Zealand

The Pacific Ocean Ring of Fire

The plates are most unstable under the **continents** and oceans of the Pacific Ocean called the Ring of Fire. These areas have high mountains and deep ocean trenches. This area has many earthquakes and tsunamis, and 75 per cent of the world's active and **dormant** volcanoes.

United States

South America

The Indian Ocean trouble spots

Two islands in Indonesia, Java and Sumatra, have a high risk of earthquakes, tsunamis and volcanoes. One of the most famous volcanic **eruptions** in history occurred on the island of Krakatoa in the Sunda Strait between the two islands. It is estimated that 36,000 people died.

Between 1907 and 2004, earthquakes on these islands killed almost 22,000 people and volcanoes killed 18,000 people. In 2010, a landslide in the village of Tenjolaya, 65 kilometres from Bandung, the capital of West Java, killed dozens of people.

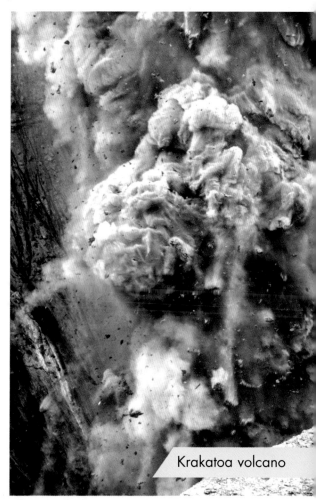

Krakatoa volcano

The most well-known disaster to hit Indonesia was the 2004 Indian Ocean tsunami, when a 9.1 magnitude earthquake triggered the enormous wave. Over 130,000 people died. This tsunami killed an estimated 228,000 people throughout the countries of Southeast Asia.

Scenes of destruction after the 2004 Indian Ocean tsunami

Instability in the Mediterranean Sea region

Parts of Italy lie on a **fault line** so earthquakes and volcanoes have affected many cities, towns and villages. One of the first volcanic eruptions recorded was in 79 CE, when Mount Vesuvius blew its top, burying the **ancient** cities of Pompeii and Herculaneum. Since then, there have been more than 50 eruptions. The city of Naples lies at the base of this volcano and up to 650,000 people live on its slopes. Any sign of an impending eruption could force the evacuation of more than a million people.

The Mediterranean Sea off the coast of Italy has many volcanoes. The resort island of Ischia is the most worrisome. An eruption there would affect Naples.

TIME LINE: Some major earthquakes

1908

A 7.2 magnitude earthquake reduced Messina, Sicily, to rubble. Several lesser strength earthquakes have occurred in Sicily in the past six years.

1980

An earthquake centred in Eboli, Italy, stretched across the country towards Naples. It killed 2,735 people and injured 7,500.

2012

Two earthquakes, nine days apart, occurred in Mirandola, Italy. It was reported that 26 people were killed and 350 injured.

The ruins of Pompeii with Mount Vesuvius in the background

The city of Naples lies at the base of Mount Vesuvius

2016

A 6.6 magnitude earthquake rocked central Italy near Norcia. It is believed to be the strongest quake to hit this nation in many years. It killed hundreds of people and left thousands homeless.

2017

Four earthquakes happened in quick succession in the same region, causing buildings to collapse. Emergency services were hampered by snowstorms and very cold weather, but fortunately no lives were lost.

Conclusion

Natural **hazards** and disasters such as earthquakes, tsunamis and volcanoes occur when the earth moves. If they occur in areas where many people live, the result is disastrous to people's lives and property.

Scientists try to warn people when volcanoes are dangerous. But sometimes **eruptions** are hard to predict. People cannot eliminate these natural hazards caused by the continual changes of the moving earth but they can take steps to reduce their impact. **Earthquake engineers** have devised building techniques and materials that resist all but the strongest earth movement. Knowing what happens when they occur helps people to prepare for them. Families and people in the community can prepare for a disaster with an emergency plan.

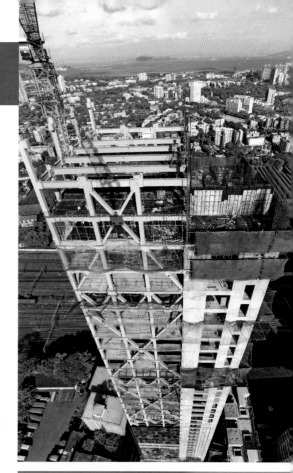

Make a plan
What do you have to consider?

Glossary

ancient belonging to times a long time ago, in the distant past

atmosphere the different layers of air that surround the Earth

avalanche a large amount of snow, ice and rocks suddenly and powerfully moving down the side of a mountain

calderas very large holes or craters formed when a volcano collapses, after the magma has been ejected

continents the seven large areas of continuous land found on Earth

dormant inactive; still able to erupt but not likely to do so in the near future

earthquake engineers people who design and analyse buildings and structures so they are able to withstand earthquakes

eruption the forceful ejecting of materials such as rocks, hot liquid rock and gases through cracks in the earth's surface

fault lines a long crack in the surface of the earth

geothermal related to the use of natural heat that comes from inside the earth

hazards causes of danger

lava hot, melted rock that flows out of a volcano

magma hot, liquid rock found under the earth's surface

tremors slight shaking or trembling of the earth's surface

Index